Numinous Byways

Numinous Byways

STEPHEN FALCONER

RESOURCE *Publications* • Eugene, Oregon

NUMINOUS BYWAYS

Resource Publications
An Imprint of Wipf and Stock Publishers
199 W. 8th Ave., Suite 3
Eugene, OR 97401

www.wipfandstock.com

PAPERBACK ISBN: 979-8-3852-4431-7X
HARDCOVER ISBN: 979-8-3852-4432-4
EBOOK ISBN: 979-8-3852-4433-1

05/08/25

CONTENTS

TO THE DELIGHT OF A GODDESS

I breathe,
you swallow

I suppurate, you ingest

I perspire,
you are refreshed

in the curve of my spine
smell the fragrance of blossom,
in the indentation of my abdomen
drink the water
welling from immeasurable depths

through my sockets see beyond the inveterate tic,
the flecks on her lips,
the lining around her lids

through inflamed eye
slumber
wakening around her naked thighs,
bruised membrane and tearfulness,
shudder and longing

unrelentingly
the sodden cloth beneath her waist.

NIGHT WATCH

If I add a piece
of chalk
to the increasing mound above me,
it will contribute to our journey
toward the sun,
the moon and the brightest incumbents
traversing the expanse above our heads.

Not that we will reach them-

the clouds exceeding our wildly grasping hands
tell us this.

As they proceed over the hills,
we will,
undeterred in our ascent,
look down on the industry of others,
who felt the same intention
to build as high as we can

out of reach
of the bones we'll become,
the corpses we'll inhume,
disintegrating

as a smile
at the day's end.

Silbury Hill
Wiltshire

DEATH DEFYING

For that moment
you forget about the world
and nothing really impinges
upon your immanence,
you can rest securely
in the notion:

an eye survives
as the body evaporates,
inwardness remains inward
until you wake up in a dream

skirt clouds and rainbows

brush past the sun.

ROCK POOL

Between the extreme absence
of vision and everything encountered,
the annihilation
of substance
and the plenum,
no sense of life
and enrichment of everything possible,
there's a place no one has signed,
a hollow where things happen
that could never have happened

where the countenance of humanity
with myth,
of animality with divinity,
and clarity with obscurity is manifesting

the surreal potency
of blood in water,
marrow in rock,
saliva in gum leaves
and plasmic quivering in light
is brought to the surface
before calcifying once more
in bones seen by ordinary eyes.

Kings Canyon, Northern Territory

OVERSEER

Secretive as a wound that heals under fur,
I'll close my eyes,
contemplate your sorrow,
ebullience and misdemeanors

the fluctuations of my heart
absent from the surface
still touching your throat
dropping into your soles,
invigorating the shudder
as you rise from your clinging wife.

While you scurry to avoid being drenched,
I'll drink the rain,

while you cower
from the heat of an unearthly orb,
I'll let it burnish my body.

When you slumber at night,
I'll stand attentive to the star's course
and the moon's journey,

when you exit like a ghost born in fading light
I'll articulate the distance
between frozen, dead eyes
and a burnished wilderness.

As you gain purchase on limpid soil,
I'll aim a live shaft at your ailing lungs

guide you into flesh.

The Long Man, Wilmington, East Sussex

WATER FOR A MULTITUDE

Although the ruler whips subjects
into submission,
spiking heads overlooking the valley
where fruit withers in the heat,
an angel touching the ground
in search of a source to purify
will be in accord
with the incarcerated plane shedding tears.

Although the viper twists around a waist,
severing lifeblood from the head
to the toes,
sweet moisture will turn black flesh
into a well

a mightier than almighty presence

born in a naked breast.

Abraham's Well, Beersheba, Judah

SHADRACH

Bare my skin
in the inferno,
bright my eyes in the intensity,
hard my bones in the fire

a bubble of blood preserved on ice,
a sliver of tissue
sustained in a raindrop,
scorched flesh cooled in ocean wind

fresh
my heartbeat in the blaze,
clean my lips in the furnace,
sure my steps in the flames

you'll walk with me by my side.

MASTER

Semi-conscious
at night,
he can smell the intent
to disarm the warrior who fends off the scourge,
sense the feral longing to snarl in every bone,
blind flesh

obscure the altar, spike hearts with fear,
goad a seer
into flight

until paring away contaminated tissue inch by inch,
he will descend
into the underworld
to incubate
in the knowledge

eventually,
light
will flood maimed organs

turn into a word within his heart.

COMPENSATION

With no intention to speak
of the ruin you may foresee,
thoroughly unconcerned
whether I live
or die,
weep or smile,
can you navigate
between the shoals of inborn outward
and out there
inward,
descry return
between pleasure anticipating an end
and the feeling I am always becoming,
yet uselessly,
still my heart in warm ocean light?

The wind
dropping to silence, birdsong
hushed in the leaves

more deeply shaded
than a rose,
gentler
than a peach in bloom

poignant than honey.

WRESTLING MATCH

If I could build your edifice
on a broken bone, would I?
If I could unfurl a flower
from an infant's grave,
nurture and water it
until ablaze with the power of the Heavens
it exuded holy fragrance, would I?
If,
in the confines of a mother's heart,
after her child
was dashed
on the rocks
and scattered on the beach,
I could create a loving couple
who beat in time with angel's wings,
would I?

Of course I wouldn't.

COMPASSION

Your breath
smelled like the underarm
of a giant ready to crush an adversary
twice as small,
your lips
tasted like dead saliva after a kill,
the grey note
you emitted
when you saw your father pass
from pink
to dull green
sounded like air escaping between the teeth
of a rival who felt the urgency
of my need
to knock him senseless.

Shall we dance?

HALLOWED

Even if I were to crush the moon
between my fingers,
the moon's light
would still shine

even
if I were to cast the sun
even deeper into inert absence,
rays would still penetrate
to the back of my eyes

even if I were to smear the stars
with black glue,
the millions of tiny bright points
would still flicker
from my pate
to my feet

for you are their source,
their continuity
and the verve
that makes them
emanate from their source—

you.

NATURAL BEING

Vast the kingdom of need,
wide the demands of love
to be satisfied, high
the urgency
to abate the clawing of misery,
deep the illusion
I have something to assuage the pain,
rectify the imbalance

I
am useless
and, too, what I have written.

Will you accompany me
for a walk in the woods?

The trees are in bloom.

CUPID

No one
can avoid my arrow,
the bruise on a heart
will linger
after the poignant tip reaches the center

only I can see who is ready,
only I am able to penetrate the mist
and let fly

with my will
to join two

as one.

ACROSS THE OCEAN

Now
as there is no encumbrance
or hard ground to pull the senses
to exclamation
of purpose,
I can move
where I will,
to where I belong

my paddle dipping,
releasing spray
in an arc meeting moonlight

without resistance,
nearing the stars as they descend
and rise
into blue black nakedness

life long as a white cloud
on a blue sky,
the impulse to die in battle
windblown as karaka on a high point,
embodiment
vulnerability of a flightless bird

indifferent
to hostility,
the scar wracked surface,
the cosmetic to-ing and fro-ing mortal pattern.

Napier, New Zealand

CRIMSON RETREAT FLECKED BY NIGHT

In spurts the last echelon finds its way homewards,
encountering eleven words
to hamper its return, bleeding over hides:

"You belong to us"

gazing at the sun on the horizon,
perspiring from naked pores:

"Your flesh will fructify in our bond"

extracting another arrow,
calling for assistance
from realms beyond mortar:

"Answer to no God in stone"

losing ability to discern our beating hearts,
checking the flow:

"Ripe seeds will putrefy in their glands"

breaking the will to confine each man
to the paradise of never-ending heat,
roving eyes, and the urge to begin over and again

another calling murmuring gently in the spine:

“One God only”

cauterizing the wounds that happen to last.

Thessalonica, Greece

A DEFINITE PATH

A holy man asked if this attempt
to cross another river
brought contact
with the hierarchy apportioning power
to the accomplishment of the task

to drive through foreign land
straight as an arrow,
ruthless as a wolf devouring kittens

suck marrow from a child's femur,
twist its hip to face east or west

for he knew the bond we make with the earth
is vital only
if the spirit permits its course,
an arch support a mass of feet
while the godly one requires order
at the expense of spontaneity,
bone and sweat
at the expense
of white clouds softening rain

hegemony
at the expense of individuality.

Guadalquivir River Bridge, Cordova, Andalusia

LIVING WATER

What does it take to stop the flow?
A growl,
a remark made in bad taste,
light
snuffed on the horizon?

What does it take
to let it
freely run once more?
The Word, silence, belief,
faith, harmony,
or merely submitting to the flow of things?
A stream,
a spring bubbling from the depths,
love?
A being greater than can be conceived
in moments of repose,
enlightenment,
simplicity,
the Messiah?

All this, and more, or—

less?

I give up

listen
for the next refreshing line

out of

nowhere.

FATHER ON EARTH

Entrusted to protect
and care for the boy
who will become the leader of a multitude
of believers touched from the horizon's propinquity
to an ethereal plane,
he'll shape his son's development
until he grows into an adult
capable of transforming a withering heart
into an enrichened soul withstanding temptation
of the evil one,
place at his disposal the skills enabling him
to carry out his appointed task
to illumine individual salvation

yet,
not merely initiate
and utter thought

but act
with the utmost intention
of bodily self.

REFINEMENT

The sweet scented lily growing through tissue,
spreading through a network
of veins,
opening
and drenching senses
with fragrance
reminiscent of its inception

immanent in pearl shine
on fingertips, dew on eyelash,
rosebud gentleness on a smile,

now that the Word
has become a man.

HEARTFELT POLARITY

In the shade of a fig tree
I contemplate
how high the leaves spread
until finding the limit
of their ability to reach the sun,
and deep
the roots grow.

Swollen with blood,
ready to burst asunder—

oblong pearls and square crystals obscuring a fall
through unfurling blooms seen with sane eyes,
an empyrean daughters' funicular torso enabling sweat
and lymph
out of pristine glands to flow
into wetlands, stagnant and silted—

solitary
against molten backdrop singeing diaphanous wings
if they descend further,
loftier and transparent in strata
that have no definitude,
will to survive,
or even piquant taste
of liquid brewed in a goddess's clean receptacle

purer and whiter
in clouds surpassing the pink tinged swirls
on the horizon,
brighter and freer beyond the sun

an embedded crucifix
in the temple reminding me
to return to its inner recesses.

John 1, Jerusalem,

I'LL GO BY NIGHT

I would erect the greatest temple,
furnish it with luxurious appurtenances
to show I belong
to the throng
who worship the One

labour to provide ornaments
that glisten
on the altar, adorn the servant
who prostrates himself
in obedience

calculate the gain to be made
from offering gifts to the higher priest
who would ensure my position is unassailable,
enact the law with authority
ordained from the impulse of history

but,
wherever I turn,
distanced
from the morning star
remembered from childhood
is the conviction:

whatever I achieve
is nothing
compared with the One
who could absolve the guilt
accompanying my every action.

John 3, Jerusalem

ONE MORE CHANCE

Offer me a moon that shall break open
and spill the water curdling her light,
in turn the sun filling her
with sacral timbres born
of luminosity:

"I will burn to the core."

and you
saturating her
with blood from an open vein

however, bone black squashed
where hooves thud
and prance,
I will gladly receive a flickering
in my marrow.

John 5, Bethesda, Jerusalem

THRESHOLD

White matter
spread from the acme to the nadir,
red encirclement,
and my eye in the center

brightness glowing from alpha
to omega,
darkening edges,
and my heart beating at the core

love transcending all this,
ardor transcending all that,
and you
and I looking at one another

warmth becoming all this,
heat immanent in all those,
and willingness to say, "I shiver"

silence within,
absence of noise without,
and a corpse lit up by an unearthly flame

John 11, Jerusalem

A GENTLE TOUCH

A vein,
a bruise,
a hand passing over an infected joint–

echoes
of brutality directing footprints,
hatred forsaking a steady course
stranded with tender soles
on red earth meeting no boundary
to the sun's ancient defiance
and loneliness,
lame steps entering ever increasingly smaller circles

allowing tension
to dissipate
in swirls following currents
of a temperate ocean.

EVERMORE

I could have flowered
like a desert rose pink to the sun's delight,
but the bruise
in my thigh
has spread to my toes.

I would have pined no longer
for honey in earthenware jars,
or ambrosia in flasks,
if the red dew on ageing olive twigs
had dripped silently to my forehead,
but corroding as ruins naked feet pound
into dust,
I must imbibe earth tainted globules
that never evaporate
out of noon day glare.

I may, should golden spiders spin webs
around my womb,
provide an enclave suitable
for a sturdy child to grow unthwarted
toward the opposite of what I am

but, like a tigress how devours her own,
I would mutilate the limbs
or pinch the eyelids closer into darkness.

"Mary."

Butter yellow
into primrose, moisture black buds
into droplet dark nodules,
candle lit shine
into lamp hidden glow

seconds rather than instances,
mountains
than peaks,
seas than oceans.

"Rabboni."

John 21, Gethsemane, Jerusalem

MORE THAN I CAN ASSUME

Emerging as from a chrysalis,
a perilous deliverance
enacted before a mass
of faces,
transforming the imperative to desist
from pulsation into direct ascension

a heart placed
where once roamed the body,
already born, conceived
before our hearts began to beat

a littoral dance
of purposeless shadows forming an awkward shape
only seldom seen through,
induced to speak, or showered
with drops mimicking rain falling on upturned lids

this side—

a diaphanous curtain wrapped around a skull,
squeezing into a network
of silver threads and grey passages

the other—

extraordinary presence
in the face of the highest of being

fatherhood beyond manhood,
aligned with who was,
I am,
after ever.

VITAL ENVOY

Like a dulcet bird's call
echoing down the centuries:

"Although you fancy our descent,
our disembodiment surpasses insight
into delectable environs,
sustained illimitably
without your encumbering
our distancelessness
from each other.

We will always be here
when the wind forces us back to earth,
curtains enclose our gilded cage,
legs wither
and wings saturate with mucus.
You suffer,
we are free of pain.

You die,
but we live forever.

You sear with anguish,
we avow:

"When the light fades
you are with Him."

Monastery of St Stephen, Jerusalem

ETERNAL PROMISE

Translate Christ into a nodule of decaying flesh,
his marrow to stagnant backwater.
Bury Jesus's heart in silt,
his liver in a compost heap.
Will they revive?

Immolate burning flesh
in lucid flame, wash slivered meat
with unstained blood.
Will they bleed into light,
excoriate
old design (perchance a new destiny)
aware under silver lidded eyes and extra cosmic filigree?

Or, coagulant above, septic beneath,
be taken in by an adoring ghoul
whose forefathers,
and theirs, ate through dry bone
to the center.
Eyeless, heartless,
a seeping brain providing the last drop of sustenance?

If not, the gentle blue light won't ignite,
the susurrating note
of calm won't resonate through black space,
sand won't begin

to warm,
nor droplets
appear between a fly's wing
and a rainbow, resplendent
with color we all know
descends from our head to our toes.

SHEPHERD

Throughout my life
I have known
I am guided beyond acquisition
for the sake of fulfilling the imperative
that conceived itself
as its own

neglected, to shrivel

feared about, to degenerate

faced fully, to rise from the ashes anew

a sense of having arrived
to discern
on the periphery
an echo:

"I have laid down my life,
I will protect
in times of distress

you are with me.

When you approach the darkening that obliterates everything
except your own image glazed in stupor,
I will tread gently beside your abandonment

and point."

APE

I have heard the calling,
felt love in the darkness
that could never absorb the proportions
of a tyrant, as you have become—
a crust on a mound.

"What are you doing here?
Why have you sought me?

To tempt with dreams of unearthly citadels
unbeknownst to impoverishment,
suppress persecution
because you care for your followers?"

I have no desire
to punish or mix blood
with grotesque beasts masticating the Scripture
that named them
before they arose
from a scarlet shadow moving upon mud

rather,
I'd have you proceed
to the source of unction
and healing, submit
to the guidance

where a broken spine resonates with music transforming the planets
in sympathy
with luminous messengers who protect us
from the disease
that would rob us of sight.

Are you with me?

I fear not,
and will watch you wither,
then contract
from the light distinguishing you
from a form sewn into an animal
perceived on all sides
by the hunter.

ENCLOSURE

Divulge what you are
when you say,
"I am."
Who are you
that imprints words,
one
after the other, in the roots
of my backbone, that addresses me
free rein and dispassionately?

I have no idea.

Only that you persist through a macabre,
grey swirl,
tinctures befuddling my senses—

revelation,
it would seem,
of nothing important, ending
in a flurry of rapture—

on,
and on without stopping,
at least, in this lifetime.

Is it you, no one, God,
the devil, a demon in heat,
providence,
light, death warmed up,
obedience
to sanity,
disavowal of evil?

Who are you?

The voice in the darkness,
a mouth in the spine,
the collocation of moments signifying meaning
I can hear

ruminations
of the Sun,
Earth's quizzicality,
Saturn's pain

a previous life talking
as if they knew me
intimately?

VISITATION

Spotless lily I plucked
and placed in a container filled with spring water

days later, beginning to fade.

the water stained green
and emitting a stale odor.

I have followed this path for eons,
a text in one hand,
and the other pointing to an abode
refreshed by starlight
and raised from a downpour
from heavenly clouds

as with our flower,
though,
the edges are brown
and the taste in my mouth a little off.

Whence the rejuvenation,
the miracle that transforms a drooping stem
into erect structure facing the cosmos?

Powder crushed from healthy bones
and swallowed at midnight,
the sun's aura vaguely discernable in childhood memory.

Copious gallons
of scared blood drenching my backbone,
the redness of sunset
and dawn bathing each vertebrae
with the flow that lights up tired landscapes
and hidden crevices.

Teardrops of forsaken eyes that see behind cracks
and fissures undiscerned
until exposed by the penetrating stare.

Black bone
between a word descrying its issuance
and the utterance divulging selfhood from perfection.

Millennium's weight stratified in darkening tones
lifted in one gift from intimate lips:

"Oracles feign restitution nightly,
sorcerers claim abundance in pulchritude.
I, however,
deign to capture the essence of why you persevere:

silence when I finish speaking,
the wake of my cessation,
the barely discernable hush
before I come to you?"

A CROCUS BLOOMS IN NO MAN'S LAND

Far
from the shore
a voice enters a girl's desuetude:

"I am so lonely.
I shall never see you again."

(An instep in motionlessness.)

"There is no end to what we can share.
We belong together—
my heart and your blood,
your heat and my shivering."

(Fists in untilled clumps,
eyes shut toward the moon.)

"See the last ship skirt the furze lined main,
listen to an open skull collecting rain."

(Edges softened
between a vacant womb
and bloated hands exposed to a rat's attention.)

“Anticipate Nubian ovulation reintroducing sanguinity
to transparent nodules,
breath into fiber,
scent into decayed matter.”

(Lying,
bleeding
as wind lashes a weeping brain
to Osiris’s recrudescent forehead).

Othona, Essex

BLESSING

I am here to guide you.

There is no journey to the center without the din
of inebriated conspirators who'd drive their vision of sorrow
into your marrow.

Blue lips chanting the same impious platitude:
"I know you. You are mine."

Listen to my advice.

Invert the cone
toward the Muse who will lose her will
to speak, her gratification,
her voice in the world:

"The crust on my skin
reveals the same wheal
an incarcerated felon scraped on my heart

drink your own nectar swirling above the clouds."

Disengage
the philosopher who would lead you
to the pit, his lineage,
his place in the grey swamp:

"Flecks in my eyesight
reveal the same characters
a prisoner
would draw on his cage

infuse
the drifting wind
with the undulation
of respiration."

Remember,
I ply the channel leading to one
who not only died,
but still abides in the veins

fathom,
through discolored waters
and sunken feeling,
a voice soft
as powder resonating with ghostly charm,
an abode light as morning sunrise
giving space to address you
at last:

"Your heart tender as a thrush's throat in spring
lifts out of slumber.

You
are free to go
your own way."

EVEN DEEPER THAN WE WOULD THINK

I would that I could train my senses to the heights,
acclaim
His presence hovering at the apex

relinquish
dependence on carnal satiety
to sustain in times of dissatisfaction,
bask in the glory of the risen Lord
purified of all craving

He
could descend
to relieve the wasteland of its lonely aspiration—

only
by its own effort guiding every act,
in defiance
of spirit and light
will hollow need
be satisfied—

rest in my bones, prepare victory over flesh

for the warrior,
to turn
and face the blood-stained eye

an inebriated fool, follow the pronouncement to desist

the serene Ghost claiming provenance over living tissue,
vivify,
despite talons that scratch the carcase
left by the way
and fangs that bite into decayed meat
left over
from the kill, the inert center

avoid brushing incandescence
with her face
on the pyre, stare fixedly
into each black opening.

WHAT WE MUST FORSAKE

Intone the Script toward the blind,
the beggar, and the thief

the valley
where the rose has acquired a shade of pink,
a wounded soul bleeding in the snow.

Follow the light illuminating the shadows,
concordant with fretful strings
drawing out a pact with one eye
and a missing finger—

the curling leaf turning upward,
facing away from the roots below—

look
expectantly toward the source of conscience,
which never lingers
for any more
than the beat
of a butterfly's wing
or an ant leg's final kick in the air

a sultry moon
falling from orbit,
the vivid dig into the heart.

Despite moisture bubbling in furrows
lit up softly,
and naked bodies swimming abreast,
stipple the ground
with tears
and sweat following prayer to His sacrifice

puckered lips,
soft petal skin
and mystical scent vitiating the deed
a holy man would aspire to
when free
to dress the wounds of a profligate
who happened,
perchance,
to be lost in the woods he loves.

BY THE GRACE OF GOD

Which hand,
red raw and losing fluid
is unable to carry water
to a believer
who washes impurities from the skin,
not unlike the Lord subjecting His immortal self
to immersion in the river.

The hand that stole the egg,
as it was sworn against him,
unable
to scratch for crumbs
and emulate the act that could show faith
is sustained

to reach out, grasp the staff
held by the hand which, in its mercy,
could touch the offender

absolve him
from guilt
had he been able,
just so gingerly,
to feel the page on which it is written:

the pure in spirit
shall see light
and the innocent be set free?

CONVERSION

If you could take an axe
and carve a rune
into my skull
it would signify

"Victory."

If I could take a splinter
from the reliquary
and plant it in your belly
it would betoken the advent
of His holy Kingdom on earth.

If you crushed my face into ice
you would claim nothing more
than an instance of bravery.

If I buried a jewel inscribed
with the letters

"INRI"

in your spine

you would eat coals with red lips,
emulate the dance
of an angel fixated on bringing wrath

at centuries old wastefulness
to ground

mindful
of the Creator, immanent
in translucent blue, cold flame,
untouched centre and ice,
extricate from your idol ensconced in blood.

BACKBONE

In winter,
when ice
has clogged the rivers
and impenetrable drifts obscure neighboring fields,
I will undertake an arduous journey
from the comfort of my woman

inch my way,
blackened with fever,
comatose near to expiry,
to the solid ridge
jutting into the clouds

incumbent upon me
to renew relations
with the guardian who keeps every door
firmly tightened,
until forced through on his command,
“Wake up,
drive forward with glittering eye

eradicate the last vestige of submissive flesh,
stamp my name on inertia
which has striven to exact its authority
on the wastelands

that recede

far away to the north.

REVITALIZATION

"Amen,"
they say, over
and again.

"Hallelujah," they cry,
even though breasts are corrupted with self-pity,
hands tainted with larceny, toenails painted
with colours fit for the devil's own.

See them pass the poor—
noses in the air

hear them shuffle
by the dispossessed,
and heap silver
on platters that could feed a colony

an eyelid
fluttering at a passer-by.

I know I dwell,
too,
with the carnal lover who embeds his pound of meat,
the cock eyed
who slavers at the sight of taut skin,
the idolator who buys his way into office

but I know,
as sure as manna
was licked by a tribe in the desert,
communion on my knees
will bypass the lurid ache on my thighs,
and clear water wash through gravel
and marble
in a tomb to daylight,
a robed coenobite will crave no flesh
and need no other word:

"You will tear from its place on the steeple
a sovereign
and replace it with the Cross."

ABSOLUTION

In spite of dark blades
seeking a moist neck
to sever, bitter herb
apportioned to an anxious day dreamer,
or a follower who has lost nerve
in the pincer movement to surround him,
the holy warrior will be victorious

he will be accorded his weight in light,
elevated on the Text
that brings Heaven into the sinews,
and the murmuring descent, toneless
but inviolate,
into the toes, "Deus Volta."

I shall surrender my limbs to the Cross,
eyes
to the steeple, heart
to the being who turned insipid self-exclamation
into the essence vouchsafed in oil
distilled in the sun—

a droplet
splashing on a silent pool,
rippling to the edges—

a dance between the eyes
into the lilt
between pink blossom,
moist liver
and worm holes.

No more to suffer at the hands of the Antichrist,
who'd prise each bone from its socket,
grind my nails into paste,
carve a name into my chest:

"Victory."

DEFENDER OF THE REALM

In my hand
I have a rose,
in my head a vision of the Holy Virgin
in labor, in my feet
the determination to conquer the infidel
for the sake
of verity and allegiance
to the Sovereign,
in my breast wonder

staring into your eyes

limpid pools

swooning,
tucking you to my side

a breath in your ear

"To the coast.
He has ordered"

"Damn him. "

"My love"

"Now,
your Lordship."

In my skull I can hear the hooves
of an army closing in
from all sides,
in my stomach
feel the bile rising at your order,
in my heart
listen to a pronouncement
that meant nothing
when you were in my arms:
Have mercy
upon the vanquished

tend to the wounded as they lay
in agony, salve their abrasions
with tenderness

bury the dead with dignity.

open your hands, catch raindrops
as they wash away the gore

steep yourself
in the silence

pray you will never again have to face an attack.

THE IRONY OF HOPE

Amid the confusion,
the spineless lack to gravitate toward the meaning
you apportioned at the beginning
an attempt is made
to raise the platitudinous into the stratum
where you can be heard more clearly

there can be freedom

deliverance.

The effort to recast parallel existence transcending dust
turns our hearts
into the pattern integrating celestial engagements
within choral relationships

eyes into windows
for your insight into earthly being

skin into the sculpted surface
protecting your never doubted sense
of identity
from the eager rush to perform great deeds
in your name.

Cathedral of Our Lady, Antwerp, Belgium

EXTRASENSORY

Are the stars an emanation
from angelic ardor pinpointing wakefulness
in an expanse that repels their approach
or, merely,
consume the core in a remorseless blaze?

Do your eyes peer only
where you direct them on the horizon

or,
impeded by the black garb enwrapping somnolence,
delectable cream freshly whipped,
effervescent bubbles emptying cool air
onto an exposed nape,
the hornet's nests under your feet,
a knife blade blunted in gristle

(your dreams
at night)
alone and fearful
of the waves that beat upon the shoreline,
and the wind that rocks your abode
to its foundations

you perceive who turns the wheel
and ameliorates punishment
for short-sightedness?

AN ETERNAL VERITY

Not merely
what you hear
in the morning or eat
at functions for the King

it remains the same after calls over millennia.

Not the web between awkward bones
or the down under outstretched wings

as the moon's glow touches the frost
on pine needles. every distance
toward a goal circumventing cliffs
is sensed.

Not the graceful flight
on drafts rising from a lake
or the swoop
to wheel beyond eyesight

when hail
has obscured the mountain
and mist
obliterated contours
seen by extraordinarily acute senses,
the uncanny ability to find one's way.

Not an egg, claw
or yellow beak
pecking for worms

the refusal
to submit
to a law that demands
each breast, feather and tail
has been created
only for the skill of a musician
to mimic its issuance
or a butcher to carve it into pieces.

A SANCTUARY IN THE CLOUDS

If I could relinquish dependence
on the earth for sustenance,
transubstantiate
the spring displaced by temporal alignment
into your blood,
unveil the solace born
from an empty recess,
and gaze with unborn lineaments
into the spring from eternal light,
I would

I serve your calling, look
to salvation
before anything else.

An uncomplicated structure on a mountain—

mist and rain encasing its heart,
brick and mortar transposing the solitary denizen,
who'd place his feet to see over the cusp,
into being just a little higher—

a conclave of consecration
decrying avid self-abundance

in sight of deliverance.

Benedictine Monastery, Montserrat, Spain

OLD AGE

A branch taps gently
against the window

I turn the page.

A leaf flutters to the roof

I mark a special passage.

Dust motes circle
in a ray of light

I make a clear note
of the meaning of the text.

A cloud obscures the afternoon sun

I close the book
and rest it
on the mantel.

The wind vainly tries to enter under the door

I try to remember
what I have read.

Cobblestones clatter
with the arrival of a guest.

Another subject will do just as well.

FALL FROM GRACE

Given
that the standard has fallen,
our blood drenched the sand

the king clouded his wit with claims
of sovereignty over the desert

have we achieved anything
where scorpions crawl,
dogs howl
and mendicants caked with disease
follow our prints begging for scraps

absorbed the earth
where the Lord walked,
rested his head and attended the sick

built a bridge for the pilgrim
who'd taste salt
on his tongue, declare
it was the same Mary shed
in the trickles making their way
to the sea that doesn't move
slake his thirst with vital fluid

(wine crushed
from the fruit nurtured within reach
of living water
scarlet as the tomb in which he lay)

or lost to the heathen
obligated in prayer to demand restitution
of the sanctuary divined as the ancient,
promised land
unto future generations who'll have no fear
of marauders encircling the soil given
to all believers to prosper on?

Athlit, Palestine

WROUGHT

I can hear the clash of metal upon iron,
see white hot coals under the brazier,
feel the sweat pour off my cheeks,
mould the elemental stuff found in levels beneath my feet
into an icon tempered in a hard,
cold stream,
original and simple

penetrate to the root
of swollen heat,
allow the mead brewed in the confines
of glistening quiescence
to pour
into each chamber.

I can taste the salt,
smell the sulphur,
withstand heat on my skin,
convinced every spark
contains the same dedication to work
as arrays the stars.

I can take the glowing rod,
with might
and endeavour
fashion it

into a pointer directing to the incarnate Word
sanguine in the core of density:

the secret ingredient
making a useful object
perform to its utmost potential.

HOMAGE TO A DYING PRINCESS

I could mistake your skin for the outer layer
of a temple, your breast
for the dome personifying the heavens,
your eye
for the entrance
to the inner void

your heart,
unseen yet palpable,
to the life
I would emulate

if every inch
of the shadow behind your suffering
were to lose weight in the flow you sustain.

HABIT

Eventually
all paving stones separating the cloister
from the chapel
will be marked with devotion

an elderly soul
who hasn't adopted the path of complete surrender
is awaiting the true voice.

Head bent, eyes unaware
of friction-

the dissonance marring earthly need-

he shuffles past an arch.

Occasionally
he will pause, cite
an unknown invocation
to an equally unknown beneficence

and move on.

DETACHMENT

The Muse would be pleased
with verbiage prefigured in patterns
that follow the rhythms
of her bloodstream,
albeit attenuated in ethereal realms

a doyen,
who provides succor
to dying females caught up transitioning to motherhood,
a litany of possible cures

the shadow,
who persists in woodland
and covers the bones
barely cognizant of their own being,
a nearly voiceless similitude
that says nothing much but:

"I am ready to receive eternal nothingness."

INEVITABILITY

If only for a half second, can I forget how I clamor for erasure,
if only in an insect's inhalation eradicate the millennia preceding,
forgo my name on works of quietude.

Silence but an ache, luminous abeyance but awareness of outcome.
Semblance of unending effortlessness vying with a pinpoint
of purpose empty as a moonless night sky anticipating sunrise.

I could listen to the drip drip drip out of a long pipe— water for a tired heart,
smooth over a wrinkled brow— ointment for a wounded liver

an unwanted ghostly sheen between my thighs while sleeping.

That second would become a little longer, surpassing a fretful denouement:

"A cross to bear." Original sin." No one can avoid weakness,
ameliorate the pain of having lost once more to the stirrings of lust.

RETURN

Candlelight on the paving stone,
footsteps outside the window

Holy Holy Holy

darkness in the corner,
scraping beside the door
Sanctus Sanctus Sanctus

a star in the night,
a film of dust under the altar
Amen Amen Amen

a virgin in the chapel,
a monk sidling beside her

Verily Verily Verily

a moist finger between her thighs,
a cloud bank forming beneath the moon

"Save me Save me Save me"

a high whisper
in his ear, "Desist"

a flock of birds
settling on a tree, snow

on a hill, an afternoon

on noon.

INTO THE WORLD

Where milk would flow from giving birth,
the delectable stream between the poetaster's simple formation
and jagged image,
she'll view the uninterrupted silence
of a lonely womb:

a garland of rose petal around a white brow,
glittering eyes and raven hair.

Instead of a cord connecting one beating heart
and child bursting forth
into warm hands
and sweating lap,
butter milk lips,
smooth cheekbones,
aquiline nose

beauty lost in reverie.

WISHFUL THINKING

Zero weight.

When my eyes and heart lift into aether,
the clouds become my footstool,
rainbows the base
for transparent arteries.

Lighthearted.

Drifting by disconnected orbs revolving in free space

they could be planetoids
or the circling thoughts
of denizens
who lost their way from Heaven:

"We accept we are not wanted,
but will return
when the Maker appreciates individual brilliance.

Untrammeled.

When ghosts, my friends,
who shriek their name loudly
are unheard,
the bells of doom silent,

and the witness to the outpourings
of suffering graciously deafened,

I know,
at last,
I have found my home.

THE WORSHIPER'S GREATEST FEAR

Wait,
listen. . .

I can hear
the words entreating
us all to follow, and
encounter singing
beyond quiescence

the virginal issuance:

immortal maker
and keeper, meliorator

substance, end of all striving

anointer, merciful,
amor, light, delight

end of all travail,
cardinal luminance
of aspiration

indefinite
without you.

Often,
I
stammer:

You'll depart,
leaving
me.

Come Down Oh Love Divine, Bianco da Siena,(Ralph Vaughn Williams, Down Ampney)

RECREATION

Oh Lord,
round my lips,
divine as I can make them.
Oh,
the full moon, the sun
glanced briefly
through smoke or haze—
a circle, like an eye
looking back at my eye—
a black round dot,
opening
and closing, letting you in,
reconfiguring
the groundswell forming your likeness,
inscribing endlessness

in your form

rebuilding you as a dome.

Florence, Italy

IGNORANCE

Old man wrinkled
and bent,
collapsing into weak bones.

Saints in haloed vestige
ready to accumulate reward—
unending bliss,
lobes
unable to remember wounds that didn't heal
for years.

Melilotus bloom
born in light penetrating membrane,
forsaken weed curling into dry tissue
and trodden on.

Petulant,
bug-eyed simpleton refusing to answer the simplest question:
"If, for a moment,
inner air is blank,
light unnoticed in its disappearance,
how do you recognize the next sordid picture
that pops in unannounced.
Is it yours?"

The cerebral doyen calculating the distance
between Antares and his skull

noughts and numbers,
the translucent glaze
on light,
moisture channeling to the back of an iris.

With no license to illuminate their origins,
no immanence
to enlighten their becoming through glittering eyes,
unable to perceive the answer:

"What,
indubitably,
brought them into being?"

BEFORE YOUR TIME

Carefree profligate
bloated with all you could have achieved,
but didn't. Ordinary soul
ready to face up to a life
shorter than how you wanted it.
Nary a breeze to flicker your lashes,
peer, solid in the light,
to the snowcapped peak on the horizon

distance
only
as wide as the space
between your coat
and the hairs on your chest.
The severe crunch
on pathways reaching the summit
ablaze with evening sun,
rapid pulse in anticipation
of bathing your heart
in the glow.

Succor,
now that you have crossed
in the ever-diminishing whispers
redolent
with pine scent
and fresh streams:

"Young once,
young once,
too."

INQUISITOR

Can I say, eventually,
decomposing matter will be absorbed into living tissue,
rise to face the brilliance of midday,
ripen
and swell into ethereal flesh,
find its way back into sublime realms

a burnished mirror reflect His own steady gaze.

"Idiosyncratic at best, heretical
at worst.
Don't you realize words have already been written
that encapsulate the full truth of divine intention?
Yours is to submit to the infallible
and not venture into ineffable presence.

"Fall down.
You are not obedient,
and wear crucifixes
when an iron glove should be clamped around your throat
to stop your squawking lies.

You are guilty of heinous sin.

I feel His scent
in my nostrils until my bones ache,

sit in judgement
with the prayer
of an alchemist to support me
in my adjudication to turn you
toward an object free of gross elements:

You are not worthy of love
or sanctuary. You dare to question
what I have upheld
to be sound
and satisfactory
to His eternal teaching.

Boil him. Mangle his skin.
Gouge his eyeball from its socket.

What is tainting, verily, the pure word,
should be cut out
and reconstituted in fire"

A NEW WORLD

With the spread of turtle dove wings
I soared over a steeple
and dropped an egg
at the foot
of the priest taking communion:

the renewal of sacrament
engendering a way forward
without the hierarchy apportioning reality
at the expense of my capacity
to see
into the light
and emanate
to the four quarters.

The moon's blade splitting a skull
and leaving a trail of brains and clotted blood:
the refusal
to adorn my pate
with the wreaths of office
and ask you to bow before me in submission.

An umbilical cord
wrapped
around my throat
and tightening as I attempt to address a passerby:

ineffable God
beyond patterns, rhythms and tones,
invariably distant but within,
enduring beyond my capacity to say who you are.

Leaping from Jacob's ladder
into dust
and swill, only to climb
and jump again—
a familiar plane that resembles the old, but different.
I have changed.

AUSTERITY

An idol
made of bone steeped in blood
held up to the faithful
is merely that—

an idol.

A tome bound in leather,
studded with jewels
and presented
at the altar,
addresses no known love
if it stands idle gathering dust

even though glossed in wonderment
raised to ardor,
has no value unless it cleanses the soul,
tenderly wounds mortal flesh
with the barb
of need for deliverance,
imprints a perfect circle in my eye,
a fluttering dove
in my breast,
a smoldering beacon on my path heavenward.

If I am to parenthesize the drips
that turn gelid and cold,
encroaching upon my light,
the distraction of pores that open
and close in scent and oil
must be at rest

any object,
no matter how appealing,
glistening in silence,
must be cast into the deep.

QUETZALCOATL'S SECRET KNOWLEDGE

Spray into the air,
nourish the plants
and seeds

sing
of lakes abrim with water fallen from the sky,
the harvest
of grain to swell our bellies,
the surfeit
of fluid that pours into a womb
and distends a woman
with progeny

pour down the side
of stones
to reach the cut opened to rinse moist fat
with life.

The disc
will not shimmer
until the pool glistening below sustains a leak
from the well in our eyes,
the moon not sink
in response to a drip on the calf
unless veins flow
with a rush
and a pulse

the stain through light
not reappear
unless replenished.

AUTHOR

Prognosticate
the worst possible outcome
for a soul trapped in isolation,
unable to rise beyond a silken roof
or even sink below the fluid in its eyeball:

fractured between impenetrable mist
and collocations of endless words
stacked one
upon the other
reaching from the back of your head
to the brow.

Envisage the end of a flame
already petering out in suffocating air:

a craterous lung
inhaling bleach and mercury.

Imagine
a world
where time has stopped
in a heart that renews its pulse
from the source
of conscience and, aware
implicitly of the origin of its impetus,

with the name given
to one who knows the name
at the beginning:

I am.

INFINITUDE

Bury me
under goblin's toes pinching dead meat,
and
below that
melting eyes brimming sightlessness,
and I'll still recover
in lustrous fields only tiptoeing can cross.

Take me to the citadel
of glittering gems,
looking down on all traversed, and
above that,
redolent in unseasonal delicacy,
I'll still find open-ended distances
only plum blossomed eyelids
can penetrate.

Deliver me to the extreme desert,
alive and dead simultaneously,
and I,
beyond living and dying,
will point to another expanse
just as ambivalent
as this—

how can you stop me?

HOLY MAN

Even a gnat's wing
is endowed
with mysterious depths—

filaments
of light quivering beyond sight

there,
and off again,
unencumbered by a pull
to the earth

somewhat akin to my fleeting breast,
unable to fall into your soul.

The robin,
too, has ways
of secrecy—

pecking at undergrowth
in search
of nourishment, a penetrating eye

scratching at dust
to enliven the movement beneath,
a curling worm

akin to its darkness,
looking into the clouds
for release from your hold
on my loins

the far, distant,
unreachable
black night

where I want to be

supernal bliss.

SCRIPTURE

I do not have much to offer,
In sufferance little to give;
But your presence shall sustain me,
Divulge the reason why I live.

It's true I don't always mean well,
Who drifts languidly by and by;
Ghosts shadowing every step,
A rough road on which to lie.

Morning sun, though, breaks in marrow,
The chilled edges receive a glow,
Despite heartache, penury, doubt,
The word incarnates here below.

Willless, unfeigning admittance,
Perchance outside, in, or above,
Through stagnating fear of blindness,
"Raise your heart, you are in my love."

Clearly, succinctly, distinctly,
Ruinous night or blazing day,
In rhyme, prose, mundane utterance—
My task, echoing what you say.

"How do you know," they'll admonish,
"It's not yours to presume a right.
What is written once will ever remain
The valid truth, to wit ineluctable light."

TO THE OBJECT ITSELF

One thing is not as it seems

a plurality
embedded in unity

one ray
made up of many colours

does it follow
holy intention will splinter
when exposed to hard evidence,
purity of insight will be received
by one as babble,
another as incredulity,
another as dogma and, inversely,
mythical antimonies that have stood for centuries
decrease in the presence
of unerring obedience to a law
that maintains coherence
in the face
of scepticism and doubt?

DELUSION

At the end,
you will lie in a gutter
and wonder how great you could have been

hunted, but protected by the few
who risk their lives to enthrone you where you don't belong.

The right of kings to rule
is only a theory.

Don't you see it?

The destiny of blue blood
is to submit to the will of the many.

Can't you fathom that?

You will erect citadels
where infants build dreams of magnitude
and bleed like a warrior
who has lost a battle

alone, but grieved for by one
who will always put your will above their own.

The interest of a nation isn't furthered
by an uprising to overthrow a king.

Isn't it possible to grasp
That the word in your skull
isn't divine insight,
but yours?

Isle of Skye, Scotland

FOREVER

Whenever I look back at the deed
which sorely mistreated me
I am behoved to remain a witness
to the fact of bestial malappropriation of power

stay here until you hear the tones
of sadness in your breast,
moans of suffering in your sinews,
cries of distress deep from my windpipe
in your clammy palms
and hollow bones. . .

I carved out a gate of iron
for your pleasure from the emptiness
of the threshold between the public highway
and your solace

now
I hover in that space to warn you

I am waiting.

The blacksmith's ghost and Judge Charles Coxe
Wrought iron gates, Nether Lypiatt, Thrupp, Gloucestershire

IN THE BLINK OF AN EYE

Just how far can feeling feel
before being brought to ground,
how high can the unfettered dove repair
before embedded in the mound.
There must be through the mist and squall
a higher, superior place,
that surely befits a wanderer,
who'd raise his soul beyond the human race.
A god, you'd say, a testimony to the light of Jove,
entranced in immaculate garb, circling whirls, I'll behove
who'll reach the glistening porticos, gateway, ecstatic, anon
where no one will regret his passing—
a Luciferic fool, ultimately, gone.

MUTUAL RESPONSE

Just as a droplet forms on a palm
when fear has motivated a sufferer
to respond
the dew on a stalk appears

the morning light
breaks over a rift in the clouds

spreads below
with one phase of heat

I am conscious
I stand alone before the idea
I am not alone anymore:

"I love you."

THE FORCE OF GOOD

I would
that I could train my senses to the heights,
acclaim His presence hovering at the apex

relinquish dependence on carnal satiety
to sustain
in times of dissatisfaction,
bask in the glory of the risen Lord
purified of all craving

He could descend
to relieve the wasteland of its lonely aspiration-

(only by its own effort guiding every act,
in defiance
of spirit and light
will hollow need be satisfied)

rest in my bones,
prepare victory
over flesh

for the warrior,
to turn
and face the blood-stained eye

the inebriated fool,
to hear the pronouncement
to desist

a ghost claiming provenance over living tissue
with talons that scratch the carcase left by the way
and fangs that bite into decayed meat left over
from the kill,
to vacate the center humming in the pyre
and staring into each black opening
on the surface
of Hell.

WHO ARE YOU?

At the end of the day, a child played with a skipping rope, a cat mewed and the baker asked the miller for his bill. Near the fountain, merrily plashing, a young man sat in a daze. Who was he? Where did he come from? "I have no answer," said the priest. "Maybe he is an angel descended from the heavens to enlighten us to our wayward nature." "Impossible," said the scribe. "This earthly object could never hope to represent the dignity and august perfection of the Holy Trinity in whatever manifestation it appears on earth, no matter what form it condescends to in order to glide over turbulent waters." "He is a charlatan," said the mother. "Look how his eyes can never catch your own. They are so distant, and smack of irreparable dreams that torture the innocent and awaken children into the lust of harpies." "Nay!" said the schoolmaster. "Let us not be too hasty. I have an answer I think will satisfy even our darker doubts as to his whereabouts in our time. Note his white hands; they stand for purity, don't they? And his fingers, so elegant and shorn of manual dexterity, speak of absence of toil that we all aspire to. And his quizzical expression intimates the question we all should ask: What will I become if I treat the innocent shamefully, denying them light and sustenance for the sake of lineage and position. Will I embody guilt that has taken for my own purpose something that doesn't belong to me?

Caspar Hausar
Nuremberg, Germany

AVARICE

For greater return your time shall be appropriated,
for a decrease in earning power your personal worth increased,
for the moon to rise from a sea
of blood
the seal upon parchment will be clamped

pestilence retained in a cage built by iron will
and brawn:

the Tigris flows
from North
to South

plugged by desire
and scheme.

For every brick laid there is one finger missing,
for every chimney issuing cinders
a gentlemen coughs, for every heart drained
of a word or gesture
there is ink on fingers tallying debts:

there is water under the wheel sliding over smooth stones

a vagabond rests by the pool
in twilight.

For every bone attuned
to the lazy afternoon's pink-white edgelessness
a few syllables scratch across paper:

there is a furnace burning molten slag

a hammer strikes the anvil
and a child winces.

Mill
Colne, Lancashire

BEAUTY

Forever transfixed with supreme desire
Her milken skin and thigh
Accustomed to Earth's hardened plain
Afflicted in waste to die,
The thin boned supplicant
With ardor for his maiden
Aware in vain of her riposte,
His heart so sorely laden.

Across the breach of mist and wrack
The clouds blown asunder
The lonely ghost follows apace,
Betrayed by silent wonder,
The immanence of mortal pleas
Couldn't gain the hour
As Mercury 'round the furnace flies,
A moth around the flower.

In breath with scent of apple
Fresh from morning luster
He recalls the voice of unwonted grace
Which forbade he may touch her,
And navigate the distance
Through the welter of a dream
Where she plies with boundless delight
The nectar sprinkled stream.

With one last loving look
Toward her radiant cheek and lobe,
Blaming erstwhile insignificant doubts
For his ascencionless heavy load,
Enwrapped in penance knowing no end
To the clamor of remorse
He slumbers alongside his greying wife,
The embalmer of his corpse.

Hathersage, Peak District, England

AUTHENTICALLY YOURS

The pattern
in the stars suggest a weak,
ineffectual soul.
How
can I break through and be a hero?

My father mistreated me
as a child,
stunted
most probably my development.
Can I reach out with fortitude
and touch the cosmos?

My brain is quite small
and cannot configure accurate specifications
needed to build a bridge
to security. What do I do then?

I can live
fully
in the moment
and truly realize that whatever I do
I am still loved
completely and wholly

transcendently

beyond the moment.

AN IMPERIOUS WILL TO RECREATE ANEW

Even if I were to transmute my leaden feet
into gilded wings that could reach the stars,
I would still need to face my face
in the morning
and count the worry lines.

For each burst of sanity proceeding from my heart,
"I love the birds and bees
and furry things crawling on a leaf,"
the tide comes in and swamps gluttonous shellfish.

Although I could dance with purpureal imps
in a timeless land bounded by no boundaries,
I still must hand over my benefits
that won't meet our daily expenditure.

In the oft heard tinkling almost reaching Heaven's ardor,
the impulse surrendering unto the higher directive enters my skull
and scorches my brain,
but the cistern is blocked and the pipes frozen.

Luminous heights,
yet morbid undulation
in silt

cosmic whispers of surprise
in love with my eardrums,
but condemnation
from my wife
for not putting out the cat at night

august penetration to the fledgling spirit
but an awkward lisp when I try to translate
for you
what I have just said in plain English

semi-conscious
and bedridden

but I still rise beyond the illness I suffer.

GRANT US PEACE

Immortal redeemer
our land is our body
that bears edible fruits
for the world's consumption

our streams
tears reflecting the unwashed bruises
of toil
hardening calluses,
scarring the windblown surface

our malady
the untilled soil
under a downpour weeping
as if the nectar in the flower's eternal bloom
would never articulate again
an ice-free spring

destiny the seeds sewn,
nurtured and plucked
by gnarled hands in perfect might,
Lord, praying:

Gather us
to receive our dues

press us
to extract our penance

scythe us to deliver the worm
from its horny outer garment

dismember idolatry
with briar whips, releasing fluids
silted by gluttony, curdling the illicit need
for tenderness in the milk
and honey
of vagary following Satan

lashing in our love.

19th Century Churchyard, Copake, New York State

NOVEL

If I have any desires for wealth, power and fortune beyond the ordinary, I must relinquish them.

If I hold a vision subjugating the menial to an ideal born from isolation from the strict provenance in the earth, I must forbid it to take root.

If I sense discord between an actual fact and my propensity to imagine circumstances beyond the concrete, I must lay down my pen, feed the sheep, tend to the sick and, should it be suffering consumption brought about by ill climate and malnourishment, stroke a child's cheek.

For the Word will pass on no transforming influence unless born out of work that ennobles humanity, the plot will not encourage a serf to relinquish his enslavement unless it follows his travail with accurate depictions of vice and attempts to subdue his ambitions, the story will never enlighten an ordinary man or woman unless it transposes art from self-enjoyment and articulation of self-wonderment into a statement that has humanity as its focus and the innate power of divine witness as its intention.

Indebted to Leo Tolstoy

AUTUMN (MICHAELMAS)

Caress my face with a blade,
bathe my eye gel before it runs dry,
affix dog paws to my heart
and allow them to scrape.

What can save me?

Dry my bones
in an electric snare,
filter my blood through violet gauze,
temper my fever
with crushed ice rescued from the tropics.

How can I surface again?

Watch leaves fade
and brown,
birds return to warmer climes,
the snake bed down
between cold sod and droplets above.
Shall I sleep and dream?

Light barely rises

tainted
with night,
the earth's crust absorbs the pulse
of warm-blooded flesh,
the horizon appears white all over.

I will ask Michael to accompany me.

INFERNO

I will put it out
when I have erased the last word
that stains the purest hope
of a nation, extinguish it
when every fibre that contaminates the warp
and woof of society
is eliminated

for I am the guardian
of higher thought who protects the Idea,
'Sentiment
has at its source the rose
of divine light,'
from perjury and decay

the anathematizer of Corruptibility,
who transposes Character
with an ecstasy
of need to blame me with folly, who puts the crucifix

now caught in flames of intense certainty
reflected in an eagle's steady gaze

first
and not last

the murderer
on the pyre
not at the apex, the hellish angel
on the periphery
not at the center

who obeys the Hero
and not Mammon

who demands we cull the jackal from our midst.

1934, Book burning, Munich, Germany

MEDALLION

The mastery isn't to stake out a piece
of tribal land and claim it
for the king
but to grant each burst
of human vitality an accolade for achievement.

The secret isn't to embalm glory
in posthumous cheers having conquered unknown warriors

but
to emulate intensely fine light
aspiring nearer to Fortune
remembered
in untutored guidance following the lead
simmering as an unbroken sunrise
over the heart.

1936 Olympic Games, Berlin, Germany

NEURAL DYSFUNCTION

Four cold matchsticks, the candle's pallor
scattered in a gust
through a keyhole,
initials—

frozen records scraped,
most unfinished–

one leaking pipe, naked,
lint free eardrums,
quilted pads, russet,
nearly erased droplets,
an aroma of red meat,
a flake of dandruff lifting and falling,
black cotton-

tick tock tick tock––

needles:

an Orator delivered by the Sorcerer's guild
to intern cosmic transformation
in an even glassier,
surreal eyeball toned deadly white

sacrificing all

for Bluten.

1940, Niederkirchener, Berlin

FUTURE TENSE

And
then,
the sunrise discloses the outline
of a retreating figure making his way
to a new shoreline.

Beneath the pier,
the shadows
are barely touched, but
it is only a matter of time.

Inscribed upon the mussels' black shell,
the wakening light:

I am the child
you thought dissolved fifty years ago,
a body that bled
in a dungeon millennia before.

I am the waves
that beat upon the shoreline,
the breaker that curls
before plunging into its own momentum.

I am the sweet nectar of dripping lips,
the ecstatic uplift of dry flowers receipt of a droplet.

I am the surfeit of nothing,
the everything of elsewhere.

I catch you unawares,
and you can read me as you are now.

I may have been you.

A SURFEIT OF PENURY

The morning sun warms the wall
Between curtains a chink of light
Is she making breakfast?

The pulse between Andromeda and Saturn reaches my feet
Umbilical bubbles pop and fizz
Will her child have the same-colored eyes as her father?

Cobwebs brushing the ceiling hang to the window
A spider slinks into a corner
I examine the crack in the glass.

IN SEARCH OF APHRODITE

You whetted me not wine nor unction,
Veridical witness my troth so true,
In your eyes I swigged the mead
Of fermenting solace— Heaven's brew.

A flame led surge past your reason,
Into the clear, and into the night,
Then reeling, cross, and last a season
Of disinterred spirit ruing all might.

ARMAGEDDON

If I could illuminate the distance between the hierophant
born out of a concoction
of red syrup, spice and morning light
and the craving I feel
to submit to a mess of womb blood,
nettle juice and mercury,
would I resurrect in the glutinous space?

"I am a Savior hoping to lead others
to righteous deliverance,
instilling my path
as the virtuous exemplification,
wanting to corner the outreaches
of serendipity,
the market of the soul force,
blaring enthusiastically:

Look here,
copy me,
follow my image,
talk, sing and construct like me

then

peace will reign."

NUANCES OF HELL AND HEAVEN

Aloof where an eggshell can't crack,
the balloon won't deflate,
and lemon scent mingles in clouds above the horizon,
I'll imitate violet lips singing of funicular highways
into needlessness

or,
daring to pump vital fluid in an arc resembling the eyebrow
of a queen who craves an idolater's muscle,
open my legs to the sun
and ache in the pain of childbirth.

Thirst quenched with saltwater,
hands blackened with fire,
or noontide essence pouring into gladsome eyes,
the firmament devoid of rubbing edges.

Princess Charm dancing by the golden lake,
diaphanous petal,
translucent butterfly

or,
perched on a sagging line,
a moth struggling to avoid capture.

INFLUENCE

A hand
that floats between intention
and abandon,
and twists back
to form an S.
An eye
that skirts the edges of brightly lit worlds
and submerges
in ink.
A voice that follows the nattering
of the tribe
and carefully follows the next word
leaping from silence.

If I had my way,
I would transfuse the blood
of Jesus Christ into my veins,
so I could tell when the Father loved me

balance a foot in midair
and daintily, yet firmly,
place it exactly on the mark
where the poet stood
centuries ago

a flared nostril catching the scent of jasmine
in an incense burner,
the star shaped flower trailing through ivy,
a pen scratching on white paper
and articulating motion that will turn into a lengthy poem.

If I could secrete the essence of Basho,
and suffuse it through my veins,
I would write clandestine matter equally impressive

only
temper it
with a heart that has swum through neon light.

VACUITY

Dissipating in ghostlike substancelessness,
merging in thankless emotionlessness
beyond commitment,
transfiguring effortlessly the concrete object
into serenity

under the auspices of hidden cherubs
effusing delight,
limpidly dreaming self-deliverance
elsewhere

ardor ablaze,
a glory too simple,
sustenance too sweet to be true

a blister in Heaven's might,
a rainbow in a child's heart,
the dulcet wind free of dust

Magician of time inside you
sleep on.

ILLICIT ENTRY

Oracles handed to illegitimate successors
to the emperor's nepotistic lineage,
pursuable only in intoxicated reminiscence
hoping to revive his excellency's mellifluous purring
and indifferent caresses.

White finger bones tracing six faint lines
on the moon—
penetration into the depths

A somnolent concubine
seeking a lover's ailing intuition
to discover the identity
of the space fed, lonely eyes
following mucus rich folds

errantly nurtured in China

cracking.

LUCIFER'S APPEAL FOR SILENCE

I dreamt we could be perfect
and touch substance
beyond human hopes
into the spirit world
where nubile angels fly.

You supposed
we could erect citadels
that embodied longing to drive nails
through boards,
hammer feet into gold
and mark each step
with blood
washed clean with sweat.

Nothing
could be truer than this

our immaculate conception

a way
into remains
of regions which fluctuate
between here

and hell

together.

THE GODDESS KNOWS HER OWN

The flow
from her toes
to the pupils in blue eyes,
sediment to lunar virtuosity,
a plenum supporting bony fish to free floating artistry

powdered lips singing praise
to the dawn:

"Oh, how I wish to open to all
you can send me:"

Marigold colored in tune
with a golden sun:

"I'll place a corona in your hair."

the blue skinned neophyte transferring allegiance
to her gown and bows:

"I'll Hide away with you
and circuit the world.
You'll come by again, swivel your hips
and plant calendulas in dust

press flowers between warm hands, stain them orange,
and perfect the blossoms
with skin from your heart."

OUT OF SORTS (OIL SPILL)

Even when tired
I still go down to the foreshore
and watch the water approach my feet.

I am certain
something is different

the sea salt tang heavier,
cloudbanks steeped in inertia

the horizon somewhat darker
than usual.

I have no use
for this modern world,
being vague
and behind the times.
I don't have radio,
live alone without many friends
and can't follow their conversation

but something,
somehow
is different

the beach is changing,
waves hardly forming

children aren't playing

I like to watch them chase their shadows
in pools,
kick spray in the wind

upend buckets
and pretend each one was a bastion
to defend their parents against unknown terrors
that rise from the abyss.

The tide will always go on though,
won't it,
bringing up treasures and depositing them
for my interest and love of little things:

fragments of shell,
drifting wood
and bones from fish
as old as me.

Something
is so different today

my toes
are hidden,
foam sticks to my ankles

the birds won't sing.

A POETIC DISPOSITION

When I am contemplating an ancient pine
she'll place a finger on my pulse
and blow into my nostrils:

"The moon's blood shines on grass
while you bury your head in fibrous roots.

Your words are stale
and change with footprints on melting snow

yours
is moonlight on a ripple,
a tea leaf in a whirlpool,
a snail's trail in summer heat."

In a cosmic blur
and often unlocatable fields,
tell her the tang of pine sap refreshes inner lining,
an unperturbable witness resonates with green
and, silent as slow growth,
the morning sun filtering through entanglement
lights up fissures
and bumps on a rough surface

ecstasy ardor in the presence
of a god,
felicity idle repose in the blaze at noon,
rise
and fall translating marrow into pith,
mucus into sticky substance,
veins into a network feeding the outer edges

underneath each needle,
the shadow bright
as the surface concealing its erstwhile state

in the distance, white clouds
upon blue upon a summer raincloud,
isolation in advance
of tears made to fall anywhere

the uncanny the hard to catch sight of
when the drumbeat ceases,
a rose soft
as a shower
and otherworldly red:

"Go back
from where you came."

MANNA

Witness a loving descent to earth:

I am embedded in your loins,
erudite in your flesh,
and, ecstatic from beyond peach juice
and wistful blossom,
discreetly incised in your heart:

I can see the reason for your cruel glance—
it was your mother's broken promise,
her refusal to hold you at birth.

Shaped like a broken circle,
tinctured green
and wavering before your eyes,
swallow my emission,
taste the heat remaining alive,
import all the blaze and let it burn your sorrow

Refulgent waves on gemstone light

high as Saturn

deep as the first kiss.

COMPANIONSHIP

I am indebted to the stars
for shaping my character,
the planets for the nuances
of action,
the moon and sun
for the wisdom I incur,
the saints and holy seekers
for guidance,
mother earth
for depth of feeling,
the higher incarnate human
from the heights— deliverance,
and you—
the blue eyes
inspiring me to recreate them
within my own.

Morning light diffused
through a network of veins,
semi opaque blotches,
each aperture unburdened of low pressure
turning to the north, east, west, and south,
as if uncontained by the climate

leaves borne on the wind
splashed by the same rain cloud,
enamored by the same force.

I shall sing along with you:

My words are the squall,
the droplets are my words
as my words are within the sleeping breast
within the grey swirl rising from the coast
within my words within the heart.

RETURN TO AN ORPHIST

You know that behind the wall,
the block of nescience,
you will find its opposite pulsating with life—
blazing light.

How do you know?

The circle has no end

darkness no beginning.

A MOOD OF SATURN

I don't care
if you blow yourselves to bits,
choke the rivers with effluent,
or benight the usurer
with gladsome abundance

but I do care,
when life has been sweated
out of a dying cousin,
you still persist
in denying my force of existence.

TO THE END

Length:

the distance from a bird singing of daybreak
to the cancer riddled suffering
a bard endures mid rhythm.

Chance Occurrence.

The instant a grasshopper flits on your face
And, predisposed to another jump,
ends up topsy turvy in oil.

Simplicity.

The denial on a given Sunday you are required
to follow a complicated liturgy
and instead, breath three syllables, "You and I."

Destiny.

An echo from past millennia:

"You are a spinner of literature—
wordsmith you shall remain,
a creature who breathes the fragrance

of heavenly lilies
and feels the heat
of forgotten dynasties below your feet.

Freedom.

Any which way but downward

an inkling to rise.

Empathy:

You reveal the center boiling like oil
in a cauldron,
cream evaporating into clouds,
the transparent shimmer
reaching from an inch below ground
through dying tissue.

The divine asks a lot of you.

ABOVE BELOW

Water bubbling up
and cleansing the downward glance
into its source—

fathoms reflecting the selfsame face
knowing no other to call out
how beautiful the other was.

At the instant of sinking
and never returning,
glutinous libido emptying speckles
into the core breeding pestilence
and vermin out of embeddedness
in a dead Muse's diaphragm,
split limbed cadaver seeping no epiphanies
of why, if not,
or, "how has this happened"?

Lift me up, please.

Beatitudinous, earthbound, barely decipherable,
yet incipiently extra worldly echoes,
shall drift into blossom scent.

Give me one more chance.

Morose lids will flutter
in vein free openings
into her surreptitious glands,
uvular vibration bring for her lemon scented oratorio,
leading with:

"In pristine meadows
I'll linger to the strains of your surrender."

A TALL STEM

Frozen embryonic substance captures eternity's wish
that we die here together
not once,
twice,
but three or four times.

A blue tinged airflow circulating seeds ready to break out
and reproduce over again

the warmth from a faraway galaxy coaxing open a foreign looking rhododendron,
allowing it to grow unimpeded
and eventually reach where the heat originated.

STARLIGHT

If I surrender,
a diabolical lady who sews cheeks to walls,
crushes my brain to a pillow.

If not,
the impulse that could never surrender
to the authority
of one who maintains an alliance
with matter below the naval

a formation behind the brightness never seen—
white that never dims,
an expanse where no one challenges its reason
for coming out of darkness

the expanse of gas from an immense conflagration,
shining made up of particles
that can be measured and described

a leap toward a plane that will never be felt,
sworn to live
or be anything other
than that which is not there.

Father Keith's reflections on the Gospel of St John Number I

"From the fullness of his grace
we have all received one blessing after another"
Ch 1: 16

AUGUST DELIVERANCE

Come to the window for a moment.
Look between the ferns at the edge of the garden
and you may see a small hen
she hasn't laid an egg
since she was born,
can't sing
and scratches paint from the bonnet
when she chases her shadow
to the reaches of chicken Heaven.

Yet
I love her still.
The stupid thing will follow me
as if she understood my desire for human company

she'll wait
then peck alongside my walk to the washing line
singularly intent on answering my requests
for an insight into her well being
with disjointed clucks and brerks.

What a beautiful day.

There she is now,
preening herself in a pool of sunlight

now and again glinting off the axe head

two paces to her left.

Reflections of Father Keith Number 2

"Do not marvel that I said to you, "You must be born again.""
Gospel of St John
Ch 3:7

IGNORANCE

I saw him on the television-
Friday,
the pompous old fool.
What nerve has he
to think we have got it wrong

wine into water,
blood into wine,
miracles
and all that stuff.

How can he sit there
and pronounce they are fake
when I know truly deep down that Christ resides in the heart
of matter and the furrows of my unenlightened soul.

What could he
be born again as

a squirrel, a spider.
a hairy thing with five arms

a face to startle a coalminer working in the dark?

Reflections of Father Keith Number 3

"Yet to all who received him, to those who believed in his name, he gave right to become children of God- children born not of natural descent, nor of human decision or a husband's will, but born of God."

Gospel of St John

Ch1:12–13

AWAKENING

A christening again

the little head,
water dripping on his forehead
and the sign of the Cross.

What lurks
in this soul?
By the looks of his mother

nothing much.

But am I to suppose any difference
with this child
and the one I saw last week.

What makes us forget ourselves
and surrender
to the power within?

Cherubic blue eyes—

what a fine boy.

Did you see that glance
of afternoon sunlight
pass over his cheek
or was it the shadow
I discerned first?

Make your choice, Boy.
and pray you feel the joy I feel
in knowing the One has spoken:

"You are on the path."

Reflections of Father Keith Number 4

"The Word was in the world, and though God made the world through him, yet the world did not recognize him. He came to his own country, but his own people did not receive him."
St. John's Gospel
Ch 1: 10

EVENSONG

The powder
on the rose petal

the deft manner
in which the wasp descends,
earnestly devout
on taking in her needs

the silence at twilight
and the inscription

"Rest in Peace"

were all lost on the moron
who ripped out the carefully tended blooms
on old man Ketchell's grave.

Reflections of Father Keith Number 5

When he heard that Jesus has come out of Judea into Galilee, he went to Him and implored Him to come down and heal his son, for he was on the point of death.
Gospel of St John
Ch 4:47

FAITH

An infection

there is nothing which can save him

I can only place my finger on his brow
and whisper, "Have Mercy."

"Why, Father. Why?
I loved him. Is there anything wrong?"

Wasted

a living shell crumpled by weights no one can see.
"I'm sure Jesus understands.
There is no need to be afraid.
I'll talk to your mother.
It is hard for her,
I know, but you cared a lot
for your friends."

Still, boy

enmity runs deep

but not enough to cross where you are going.

OUT OF BOUNDS

Am I to hear ghosts court violet thrushes,
elevated nearer to scriptures entrapment
in perfection,
avoid consequences
of life affirming decisions,
now that I have eloped
with the eternal outsider
nourishing disinterment.

Since I joined you,
desire's thick lidded priest
served goblets steaming sweet mucus,
every time I steered milk white concupiscence
to upper echelons resisting forceful entry,
four bells tolled:

"Dance with me
while chance is still timed
to reflect irresponsibility,
caress my aching nakedness
with blue numbed fingers,
idolize me as I turn my cheek
to the vernal haze

irrigated by delight,
imbibe vulva sweet divulgence.

I can barely make out your corona
encompassing lukewarm skin,
buttered notes escaping elongated lips,
a white gown fluttering side by side
with cirrus clouds—

summer's extraterrestrial ascent.

I see you as a blush
in sympathy with ripening rosewood,
gossamer entwining filigrees
bound to tears,
a transparent veil on ice

ask you
to quietly reveal a purer poet
who still glides beneath us.

PEALING IN THE MORNING

The gladness of summer—

sarcophagine countenance
embellished with merciless simpering
and intoxicated grinning,
now that I have surrendered
to perpetual enjoyment

a blind, habitual drunkenness

the inebriated fool slithering beneath the winging toward the sun:

"Obey me as I curdle,
like an open scar tricking through melted cream,
your brain in the sweet sanguine call:

Follow me,
I can deliver you
without hearing who you are
and who you can be

one
with the indefinite singing,
circumspect trilling,
and ringing that praises Lucifer's triumph.

IT COULD HAVE BEEN WORSE

The grit caught in the back of my eye,
the splinter embedded in my backbone,
need to be washed out.

Could I dislodge them with an overture
to light,
a semblance of the sun's vast aura,
or dislodge them with a cry
into flesh,
an anointed heart accepting the flow

remnants of forgotten eons,
foreign elements glinting upwards in isolation:

sustenance gorged on a milk-stained bed,
devil's snot coughed up,
dung spread to engender one blade,
the slew of invective launched into a sweaty anvil:

"We'll tie cords around your liver
and drag it out.

As you play wantonly
into dead wind,
each supplication addressed to the golden mirror
will reflect a far way look to every snake,

lissome creature,
and worm that recedes
from the carnivorous mouth gaping in its hole

faintly,
over generation after tomb lit inertia,
bearing the shadow's initial twist of fate,
flecks will be inserted into an unhealthy,
unborn iris

before waking up
and seeing the irritants
out of focus."

"YOU"

Above water holding your breath
against the tide before you sink,
in the light where no one else
can appear
yet burning just as fiercely,
amongst the flotsam
stranded until a salvage vessel
picks you up from the debris

a violent storm's will
to flatten random abodes,
a zephyr mildly brushing a perturbed brow,
the lift and lull
on a Sunday afternoon,
impressing nothing upon a bare back

the transcendent otherness
only intimating its being
in a second of ardor,
the glare from the underworld
freezing a bone in anticipation
of arriving on time,
the puissant warrior
shuddering under the scythe,
expressing hatred for the aberrant wielder:

one who doesn't have a name.

ALLUREMENT

The puissant nightshade lover's kaleidoscope eyes,
perpetual smile
and effervescent lisp:

"You could be at home with lotus petals enfolding,
pristine warblers echoing
and extraterrestrial witness to ears descending.

They could bring an even brighter torch
to light up your eyes,
ethereal tunes to saturate your ears,
eminent phrases to burn your open heart.

We could kiss you again
and turn water into the finest champagne

as the seconds pass,
allow you to fly.

Take no notice of the disease
which cannot penetrate
where words are formed.
Don't be scared
by a demon's cry for longevity,
you will last longer than he.
Assume no guise
than one who reads the lips of ancient deities

their bodiless rumination,
charisma, presentiment,
mellifluous lines.

We could encircle your radiant forehead
with wind listing from shadowless acres,
vivify the tender spot under your sternum
with a wink of our gracious lids

softly line your nest, hidden though in timelessness,
with blossom,
leave your aching vestibule ajar
for one who could leave eons upon oceans,
millennia within raindrops,
centuries in a moment ago

slumber for eternity.

OUT OF THE ORDINARY

With translucent glaze for white porcelain,
we'll take our brushes
and gently swathe each contour
until the surface reflects the source:

a fallen sovereign,
who should have stayed
where his subjects
were clutching soiled cuts
and sickening organs,
wiping away the grime,
enabling them to see his tender eyes

where the sand is shifting,
haze clings to the reef,
and waves pound the shoreline,
a solitary figure slipping quicker
than he can gain a foothold,
descrying, at least,
a veiled moon
that inspires him to ascend.

TREASURE

What do I want to do?
Know how of the why
knowing through the how
to the way of the why without the how?

What do I want to create?
A transcendental eye that bores into hell?
Chiffon wisps spinning longingly
into Pluto's solitude?
Drops secreted quickly
as a torso climbs even further
into Andromeda's dying heat?

Can I be drawn into a creature
who means to elevate on the shoulder
of every saint,
unveil immortality
at the cost of knowing for whom the bell tolls

eye to eye, nose to nose,
brow to brow,
incarcerate in its blood,
follow its line, cling to its tomb,
and fade with its body passing by?

Keep to the wooded path

oblivious to the violet flush
on distant hills,
allow the weeds to proliferate

they have no use,
but you'll love them

their pointlessness,
capacity to strangle the purest white growth,
toxic odor

insignificant little flower,
which on close inspection looks like a star.

URANUS

I'll simply wait until she tells me how she feels.

A worm could twist toward light
containing an aphrodisiac revivifying each nerve
of a swimmer upstream,
a toad shimmer before the structure
that holds Heaven's minstrels
in accompaniment,
but I can see only as far as I am allowed

the distant glow
always appearing as my only accompaniment.

Slow as death desiring inertia,
clear as ice water on transparent metal,
quiet as dusk turning into twilight,
I am beyond the soul you feel in the heat
of the moment

Unobserved by weeping adolescents
and embryos touching the skin
of their mothers,
hardly nascent
in the extrasensory blue note
I emit to uninvited visitants past my aura,
I'll still influence every broken heart
with a newly discovered sense of renewal.

QUIETUDE

Like a phoenix restored in fire,
the vernal master
who imbues each blossom
with vigor,
a tinge of pink,
and long lividness,
I'll move toward the moon dripping ice

a past that no longer seems so distant:

a high born enamored with T'ang lyrics,
jade earrings,
a perfumed terrace

notes on a flute rising with chants
from outlying temples,
raps on drum skin awakening the dream
in the center,
plum scent following her wake
to the iron clad well

swollen eyes,
red rims,
and tear drops rising to my brow.

"Although a benign eye
would hover
like a moon douching an unholy act
with liquid light,
I'll wedge willow bark between floorboards
to prevent a sound.

Although I could involve my own longing
in his abandonment of caution,
and sustain his plans plan to tie knots
in the fingers entwining our feet,
and pulling them to his maw,
I'll quell the urgency
to evoke images grounded in the past.

Although a softly spoken warrior vows
to prolong unearthly trysts,
he'll meet a sharpened nail
at the pass between netherworlds."

FEET ON THE GROUND

Coruscating pupils seeking an abode

effervescent in copious moons
hollowed by generations leaving light
to bubble outwards,
pristine beyond oracles rendering inebriated facts
of life
only a heightened neck could reach

ice melting where hot feet glide,
egg white curdling on a hot palate,
jelly liquefying under a noon day sun

playfully, mercurially, whimsically,
in deference to blue shadows
and pink snow drifts,
lifting in rubicund skeins,
drawing even further

dancing, little puppet,
away where blindness is insight,
calumny a gentle touch,
and absence of sensitivity a godsend

and how I would drag
at your disappearing toenails,
splice my fibula with your shins

pour salve into the sucking vastness.

FORMULA FOR SUCCESS

Orienting to the sun's perpetual motion reaching beyond the stars,
transmogrifying dust into immortality,
seeking Heaven's bodiless sublimity,
you'll have no position in oblivion

scribble characters on paper marked with ink
that splashed through negligence,
orientate to the flower
and the space between the leaves
as if your own breath evinced their rising
and falling for generations
elucidate the steps of your arrival
in the mother, the child,
the wind, the storm

express how each bead
of sweat
and each raindrop finds its way back
into the same ocean.

WABI

The cherry blossom opens in faint morning air,
the scent intoxicates the nostrils
of every creature
who deigns to pass through its ambience,
and I look upward through a maze of light and shadow
to where,
unperturbed by blue spider's thread and sticky pads,
goddesses vie for prominence,
while their consorts readily submit to them.

Bones lie scattered on silver platters,
a heart pumps red fluid into tori gates, and you look on grey pulp
and shimmering veins
confined in a skull.

Anamori Inari Shrine, Ota City, Tokyo, Japan

QUIESCENCE

The dance suspended
in ink, momentum
upheld in unmoving blue

transition restrained in a dewdrop,
virtual silence
circumscribed in absence of tone

consciousness
inconscient of consciousness,
parenthesis holding no center

empty pools
overflowing waterless ocean.

What is to stop me from plunging?

THE BABY BOOMER NEXT DOOR

There would be nothing when you removed the ash

the blue chill that crept from my palate
to the blood blister upon my toe
would fade, the limpid stream
between Antares and the nebula facing Orion's intensity
revert to a painless black

the focus of dreams pass from a body
that waivers between blamelessness and absolution
from repercussion gainsaying the reward
expected from effort
to a Forever
that no din, cancerous tissue
or self-harm could penetrate

and the words of Christ, Buddha
or the soothsayer from the temple
in the city
who have crossed,
so they say, and returned,
shouldn't alienate the faith I have decided on

on my own

without holy figures prognosticating what will happen
when the phases
of the moon resist the turning sun.

ROMANTIC MAN

Find a place to escape
and remember how we used to go for walks on sunny days
when you with your moist lips would find mine.

Afternoons without desperation
or intense need to guess the other's intention
we'd simply caress and wonder where it would end,
if ever.

Evening before firelight
we'd assume no one ever before
felt the way we feel,
heard the things the way we hear

touched the way we would

the way we knew would last until every star assumed our brightness
and sensitivity.

My love for Gary McFarland, 'Thanks but no Thanks' 1968, New York City

A MODERN TEXT?

I read each story avidly: the parables, the wisdom, the action which could transform a heartless oaf into a loving human concerned with the welfare of others: timeless, insightful, sure of destiny that would realize a profounder outcome for the individual and society but in the desert a new text was discovered attributing itself to the same word:

It is before you, around you, ever-present and discernible where the leaves rustle, the sun shines on pavements, water laps against the pier and in the rhythm of speech, the lull and lift of a smoking afternoon and the tepid dreams of a sweet hearted lover finding a message in waves rolling onto the beach

It is in the light that transfuses the immediate appearance of a complete stranger who only has to beckon you onward till you find that everything is illuminated from within and understands what you ask of it

Gospel of St Thomas translated into English 1959

STALEMATE

The might I thrust
to ensure she stays within reach
is the same might she thrusts
in order to leave,

so I will claim her,
drop her
and spear her with aching blood
pumping into the night.

ACUTE MISMANAGEMENT OF A PERSON'S BOUDOIR

Eons ago, a beige neckerchief dripping blood—
a nose broken

Now,
curdled by the sight,
numbed in fear of turning devilish.
And the mothers
and fathers of silence buried their child
in sand,
since she couldn't speak proper English,
that their little daughter
was so afflicted
and so painful
they ran for cover in a big city searching for inspiration
which never came,
never mentioned a word about love,
never adored her violet eyes.

SELF PORTRAIT

I'll take up my brush,
longing to see you briefly
near the fountain passing by remnants forgotten
and buried

faintly trace the swell of your breast,
the curve of your thighs,
the lines of your hand

with deference to our ancestor
who enabled veins
to flow
with the song he raised to Heaven,
feel your reluctance
to pierce the film surrounding the mystery

embody tenderness open to the summer

as morning breaks over the moist contours
of a land
that has barely begun to flower,
approach one
too frightened
to tend to the wounded on the field.

A SAD ENDING

Unsure
of light within,
I'll look to the mud.
Unable to isolate the shadow
and the breath from glistening resilience,
I'll turn to heavy clouds.
Incapable of distinguishing between tears
and the spring which precedes acceptance,
I'll allow the rain splash against my face
and the wind blow me into shelter.

MAYBE JUST MAYBE

A poster on a billboard advertising a visit
by a renowned psychic
who will advise anyone who cares
to accept in reverence
and joy the capacity
to engage with angels
who only have the welfare
and best interest of humanity
for their ultimate meaning.

Some go by and scoff,
angered at such chicanery

others,
bemused by the claims of holistic therapy,
place ultimate trust
in the advances of medical science

but one,
unable to distinguish the lead
in his joints
from mumbling in the streets,
from his bar stool in the corner, asks:

Could she be so corrupt as me?

What have I got to lose?

ECHO

My toes smell of eucalypt squeezed in rain.
My eyes are black
as night surrounding the moon, my skin dark
as sulphur burning in ash, my brow
broad as a mountain ledge frowning in pain,
my teeth hard as opal crushed by ancestral feet.

I am a man
and she is my heart.

We bleed a youth into light
and a child into sand and stone.

And you stink of swamp water,
faeces
and sperm I cannot drink.

Adelaide, South Australia

DIFFERENCE

My dream
is of enemies spreadeagled on the ground
and dull eyes looking upward
from the loss
I experienced in encountering the sword
the last we met

each blow remembered through the skin
and throat,
each gesture of defiance
in the backbone
and each surge of bile in the heart.

As the pulse diminishes
I'll never forget your abominations and cowardice
the time you had the upper hand
when, at sunset,
wielding a bone like a knife
you opened my veins to release memory:

enemies
spreadeagled on the ground

the glutinous cough always preceding music
in the skull accompanying a dance
upon sharp stones
within grass that knows no rain.

MAGNANIMITY

A vocal swell in tune with heartbeats of thousands.
We will not be defeated
by pride."

A hand in mine
and footsteps echoing upon asphalt. "Reconciliation."

A gentleman
with a button calling for the eradication of poverty
and others unanimously declaring humanity
has no boundary to its capacity to give.
"All can share
in the wealth of the land."

There are no dreams
that can be contaminated
with fear if we, with one voice,
shout that we are in accord.

"I am alone
only if I choose to be.

I suffer if I leave you by the wayside.

2000, Sydney Harbour Bridge
Australia

UNFURLING

The spider listens to the wind,
stretches its legs to touch the clouds,
catches a raindrop on its back

and I vibrate to the tune
of fallen leaves
adrift on the river.

OUT OF RANGE

An empty shell
detached from knocks
on fair skin
or even fertile tones
where the Nile wells in Spring,
or even more distant
when the sun will burn a little less brightly,
and Saturn's in reach
of interested spirits, will neither mingle
with the Word incarnating in blood
or,
barely audible,
repeat answers
we know can be answered.

ANSWERED PRAYER

Anything outside this cacophony—

an iota,
an instant, a fleck,
a glimmer
not necessarily abundant.

Imbue
the secret recesses with otherness,
transpose meaninglessness
unable to rise out of this,
that,
there, when,
how
or anywhere.

Empty,
nix, indissoluble.

En arché born.
Spirit indubitable.
Christus.
Immaculate perception.
Reborn,
I'd stretch the wind between your wings,
lasso it into a curl around my heart,

hear you at last:

"I love you."

www.ingramcontent.com/pod-product-compliance
Lightning Source LLC
Chambersburg PA
CBHW050143170426
43197CB00011B/1950
* 9 7 9 8 3 8 5 2 4 4 3 1 7 *